Strange Creatures

and Other Poems About Life

MARVIN DRUGER

NEWMAN SPRINGS PUBLISHING
320 Broad Street
Red Bank, NJ 07701

First originally published by Newman Springs Publishing 2022

Book Cover Illustration by John Norton

ISBN 978-1-68498-201-1 (Paperback)
ISBN 978-1-68498-202-8 (Digital)

Printed in the United States of America

To Patricia Meyers Druger (1938–2014)
Her technical support, inspiration, and
love made it possible for me to write this
book and to survive and prosper.

Contents

BEASTS, BUGS, PLANTS, AND NATURE

You Can Write Poems Too

Preface

The inspiration for this book of poems arose several years ago. I was reading a children's book to my granddaughter, Lindsey. The book was terrible. Yet it was a published book. My thought was, *I can do better than this.* So I started writing poems about life that would be appealing to children and adults and would be sprinkled with humor. I tried to hire a professional illustrator, but I didn't like their illustrations. In my mind, I had a vision of what each illustration should be, and the illustrators couldn't match my vision. So I decided to do all of the illustrations myself, even though I believed that I couldn't draw. A professional illustrator later asked, "Who did the illustrations? They're great."

How was it possible for me to write a book of poetry and do all the illustrations? After all, I am a biologist and a science educator, not a writer of children's books or an artist. The answer is consistent with my philosophy that everyone is different and has unique talents. Everyone can do something special that nobody else can do. Unfortunately, an individual's talents are not always expressed for a variety of reasons. I was fortunate to discover that I could write poems and illustrate them, albeit the illustrations are childlike but appealing. Humor is an important aspect of many of the poems.

This book about life is also intended to encourage readers to reflect on their own life experiences and write their own poems. Sample poems by my grandchildren and some blank pages are included at the end of the book.

So read, experience, laugh, and enjoy *Strange Creatures and Other Poems About Life.*

Marvin Druger, Professor Emeritus
Biology and Science Education
Syracuse University
Syracuse, NY 13244

Acknowledgments

Many individuals contributed to this book in some way. Many people provided new thoughts that were transformed into poetry. Others, too numerous to name, contributed technical support. So thanks to all.

OVERVIEW POEMS

A Mystery

A mystery is something
That we don't know much about,
It tells us there's a puzzle
That we need to figure out.

What's in this book's a mystery,
But I'll give you a clue,
There are poems that make you think
About the things you do.

But the only way to really know
What the poems have to say,
Is to turn the page and read them
And have a happy day.

```
        V
  O         L
      E
```

The Magic Pencil

Sometimes when I sit alone
And have nothing much to do,
I use my imagination
To create something new.

I thought about a pencil
That could do amazing things,
It could write all by itself
And it could fly with wings.

Words flowed from the pencil,
Every sentence had a rhyme,
The pencil wrote the words
And new thoughts appeared each time.

Whenever thoughts appeared
The pencil seemed to know it,
Many pages of its writing
Turned me into a poet.

The Play of Life

The play is ready to begin,
The audience is here,
Everyone is excited,
The starting time is near.

What is the play about
That so many came to see?
Is it something sad?
Or is it comedy?

The actors tell us
What we want to know,
Poems about life
Are what make the show.

Strange Creatures

An elephant is big and strong,
Its ears are large, its nose is long,
I laugh to see its funny face,
Its body seems so out of place.

But then I think how it would be,
If the elephant studied me,
My face is thin, my body's tall,
My head has hair, my nose is small.

The elephant would laugh to see
How strange I really seem to be.

Even Stranger Creatures

Each living thing is different,
There are no two the same,
There are countless shapes and sizes
And each creature has a name.

Strange creatures do exist,
They are found everywhere,
Some live in the sea
And some fly in the air.

Some have funny names
Like kangaroo and octopus,
Elephant and chimpanzee,
Vulture and rhinoceros.

There are even stranger creatures
That have never yet been seen,
You can invent these creatures
And make them mild or mean.

So on the page that's opposite,
Draw even stranger creatures,
Make sure that you include
Their even stranger features.

The Winds of Life

It was a mighty storm
With lots of wind and rain,
They told us later on
That it was a hurricane.

Two trees were standing there
While the wind blew through the town,
I wondered if the mighty wind
Would blow the two trees down.

One tree bent in the wind,
The other just stood tall,
The bending tree stayed standing
While I watched the stiff tree fall.

When winds of life blow on us
We should stand strong and tall,
But if we bend a little
We may do better after all.

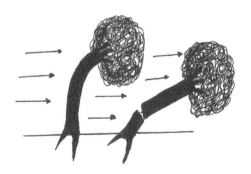

Time Marches On

Clocks are made to tell the time
And what they tell is true,
Time moves on with no regard
To anything we do.

When I'm very happy
I'd like the time to last,
And when I'm sad and gloomy
I want time to go fast.

But even if I break the clock
And throw its parts away,
Time will still move on
And bring another day.

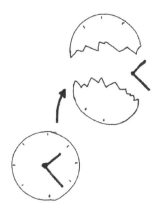

Saving Time

People like to save
Many different things,
Pennies, stamps, and bottles,
Comic books and rings.

But I save something else,
That's very hard to do.
What I save is TIME,
And you can do this too.

Do everything much faster,
You use less time that way,
And with the time that's saved
Enjoy more of the day.

More Time

Nobody has time to spare,
Time is quick to disappear,
But I can make the time return,
And this is something you can learn.

My secret is an hourglass,
It tells me how the time will pass,
The sand runs down as time goes by
And fills the bottom very high

And then I turn it all around
And that's the way more time is found.

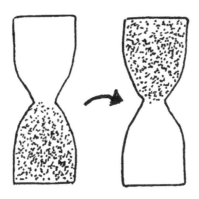

Procrastinate

A big word is "procrastinate,"
It means that everything is late,
Whatever I must do each day,
"Procrastinate" means I delay.

Though I intend to finish fast,
What is first is finished last,
I can't seem to change my fate,
Which seems to be "Procrastinate."

What's best that I might do I've heard,
Is still delay, but change the word.

Circles

A circle has no ending,
It has no beginning too,
If I run around in circles
I end up nowhere new.

Circles have no bottom,
Circles have no top,
If you want to find an ending,
There is no place you can stop.

Circles last forever,
They never seem to quit,
But this poem is not a circle,
It has an end… and this is it!

$100 Bill

Sometimes when you need a lift,
I'll be there for you,
Put me in your wallet
For a time when you feel blue.

Then feel free to spend me,
Buy anything at all,
Spend me at the grocery,
Or spend me at the mall.

If you choose to save me
For a rainy day,
Then I'll stay inside your wallet
Until it's time to pay.

Today

Today I plan to have some fun,
I'll dance and jump
And play and run,
Then I'll eat my favorite treat
And settle in my armchair seat.

I'll read the book I like so well,
The one with happy tales to tell,
But before the day will end
I'll meet with you, my favorite friend.

And one thing more that I will do,
I'll hug you and you'll hug me too,
Then at night I'll go to bed
With happy thoughts inside my head.

The day was long but full of fun,
And now to sleep, the day is done,
Tomorrow is another one.

Curtain of Life

The curtain opens,
The show begins,
Much excitement,
Music and dancing,
Talent expressed,
The show ends,
The curtain closes,
For some,
Abundance of applause,
Bouquets of flowers,
For others,
The curtain just closes.

Arrows

Arrows point the way to go,
The path is always clear,
Arrows tell us how to get
From here to anywhere.

I found an arrow in this book,
It's right here just below,
I couldn't think of why it's here,
But now I think I know.

The arrow points to the right,
So you should go that way
And keep on turning every page
And read more poems each day.

Then you will have some thoughts
That you've never had before
And after reading all the poems,
I'll bet you'll ask for more.

READ ON...

STRANGE THINGS

Reality

Are we really what we see?
Are you you?
And am I me?
And is she she?
And is he he?
Are we all that we can be?

Absolutely Relative

How thin is thin?
How tall is tall?
How short is short?
How small is small?

The only thing we seem to know
Is if you're small, then you may grow,
Or if you're thin, you may get fat,
But we can't tell much more than that.

'Cause tall and small are relative,
And so are short and thin,
What they mean depends upon
The place where you begin.

Gravity

I jumped up high into the air
And asked, "What am I doing here?
Will I keep going to the top?
Or will I ever have to stop?"

Soon I stop my upward flight
And wonder if I'm going right,
I stop up there and look around
And then I drop down to the ground.

How nice it was to be so high,
For just an instant I could fly,
I tried so hard to float in air,
But nothing seemed to keep me there.

Some other time, I know not when,
I think I'll try it once again.

Different Tears

I cry when I'm happy,
I cry when I'm sad,
I cry when I'm lonely,
I cry when I'm mad.

The tears from my eyes
Run straight down my face,
They drip on my clothes,
They're all over the place.

When tears start to flow
I'll catch them some day,
To see if they differ
In some magic way,.

For maybe the tears
When I'm happy or sad
Are different from tears
When I'm lonely or mad.

Toys

Toys can be most anything,
A doll, a car, a piece of string,
Toys are with us every day,
They are the things with which we play.

Sometimes it's just fun to see
How many things a toy can be,
A box can become a house,
A toothbrush can become a mouse,
A feather can become a bird,
Nonsense can become a word.

Our minds can make an object be
Whatever we would like to see,
So we should never have to fear,
For toys go with us everywhere,
Our mind decides what is a toy
And makes toys things that we enjoy.

A Whisper

A whisper traveled through the air,
I strained my ears to hear it,
But the message that I heard
Was not heard when I got near it.

I wondered how a whisper
Could so quickly disappear,
The wind had blown the whisper
To another place somewhere.

And somewhere someone listened
To a whispered mystery,
The words made someone laugh,
But that someone was not me.

I tried my best to catch it,
I followed it around,
But when I finally reached it,
It no longer was a sound.

So please speak loud and clear,
Let your words ring out,
Then I won't have to wonder
What your message is about.

Foosingers

You've seen a triangle, circle, and square,
A rectangle, pentagon, cube and a sphere,
But I'll bet that you have never seen
A foosinger shaped liked an alakazeen.

An alakazeen is such a strange shape
That it makes a foosinger look like a gazape,
Gazapes are long and they're circular too,
They twist on themselves like an alakazoo.

So alakazeens, alakazoos, and gazapes
Make foosingers look like a large bunch of grapes
And so when a foosinger comes into view,
You'll know that its shape
Is something brand-new.

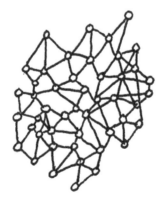

East to West

As I travel East to West
The hours start to change,
Getting there before I leave
Is really rather strange.

    It seems the day gets longer
    As I travel with the sun,
    I leave the East at lunchtime
    And eat breakfast when I'm done.

If I keep on going West,
Will I ever see the night?
Or will daylight be forever
And keep nighttime out of sight?

    I want to know the answer
    So I'll keep on going West,
    If I find a spot of nighttime
    I'll stop right there—and rest.

Soft and White

It was trapped inside a box,
But I would set it free,
I tugged it very hard,
'Til it popped right out at me.

It looked just like a cloud,
It was soft and white,
It rested in my hand,
It was a pretty sight.

I held it to my face,
It had an odor like a rose,
But when I tried to smell it,
It rose up and blew my nose.

My Shadow

I saw my little shadow
And said, "How do you do?"
I looked for you last night,
But there was no sign of you.

Now it is the morning
And with the rising sun,
You appear from nowhere
And grow to be someone.

You follow me around
And stick to me like glue,
But when the sun is overhead
You disappear from view.

Then in the afternoon
Again you can be seen
And I begin to wonder
What all this can mean?

When I know the answer
I will let you know,
But so far, it's a puzzle
As to how you come and go.

Upside Down

There is a land…
Where good is bad
And up is down
And sad is glad.

Where push is pull
And out is in
And loose is tight
And fat is thin.

Where north is south
And east is west
Where cold is hot
And worst is best.

Where lost is found
And white is black
And work is play
And front is back.

If I can ever
Pass that way,
I'll laugh and cry
All night and day.

Smart Computers

Computers are so smart
In everything they do,
You simply push some buttons,
And they bring the world to you.

Computers know most everything,
They're amazing in that way,
They give us lots of knowledge,
And play games with us each day.

I wonder how computers work?
How did they get so smart?
Do computers have a brain?
Do computers have a heart?

How do they think so fast?
Why do they click and whirl?
'Cause inside each computer
There's a clever boy or girl.

People and Behavior

Tininess

If I was tiny, I'd be scared
Of people big and tall,
I'd try to find a hiding place
And hide away from all.

But when I start to think of it,
Being small is not so bad,
It doesn't take much space,
So I shouldn't be so sad.

For tiny as my size may be,
I've lots of personality,
So even though my size is small,
In lots of ways, I'm big and tall.

Lazy Lee

Lazy Lee just liked to rest,
She sat around all day,
Whenever there were things to do,
She looked the other way.

Then one day an earthquake came,
It shook her where she sat,
One eye opened lazily,
She whispered, "What was that?"

The buildings shook and fell,
Trees crashed to the ground,
Bricks and wood and glass
Were scattered all around.

But Lazy Lee just yawned,
She did not have a care,
The world around was crumbling,
While she rested in her chair.

Finally, came the silence,
The earthquake now was gone,
But Lazy Lee still rested,
Never knowing what went on.

Lazy Lee missed all of life,
The worst things and the best,
Was it wise for Lazy Lee
To only sit and rest?

You Are Special

People are so different,
No two are quite the same,
Even twins are different
And have a different name.

So it's really nice to know
That no matter what you do,
You are very special
And you are important too.

Beauty Inside

Everyone is different,
No two are made the same,
Each one has special features
And beauty has no name.

Eyes and nose and mouth
Are all a different kind,
What someone thinks is beautiful
Is only in one's mind.

What we look like outside
Is something we can't hide,
But what really makes us beautiful
Is the beauty that's inside.

My Turtle Shell

Turtles are so interesting,
Their movements are so slow,
They have a heavy shell
That they carry where they go.

Whenever trouble comes their way,
They hide inside their shell,
No matter what the trouble is,
They hide from it quite well.

I wish I had a magic shell
To carry at my side,
Whenever trouble comes along,
I'll crawl inside and hide.

My magic shell is in my mind,
I think bad thoughts away
And just like turtles in their shell,
I'm happy every day.

Words

Words are sort of fun to use,
They also can be strange,
Rambunctious, rambling, elevate,
Ambitious, stress, arrange.

Words are an important way
To tell the way we feel,
They help us tell to others
What's fantasy or real.

Words can act as weapons,
They can hurt and sting,
They can make you laugh or cry,
They say most anything.

So think before you speak,
Let words come from your brain,
For once they've left your mouth,
You can't take them back again.

Feelings

Everyone has feelings,
They tend to come and go,
One day we feel great,
The next day we feel low.

Words can hurt our feelings,
They can stab us like a knife,
We try to cast them off,
But they affect our life.

Sometimes we're insulted
When no harm is really meant,
We misinterpret words
That had no bad intent.

So we have to realize that
When someone's words come out,
There's no way to recover them,
That's what insults are about.

The way to conquer feelings
Is to know they shrink or grow,
So whenever we feel hurt,
Just let those feelings go.

Walking

When I travel very far,
I can go by bus or car,
I can go by boat or train,
I can even take a plane.

I can go most anywhere
And find a way for getting there,
But there's one way that I like the best,
It's much more fun than all the rest.

Although this way is not too quick,
It's the one I'm quick to pick,
For I can stop and laugh and talk
And that's why I would choose to walk.

There are many people I can meet,
When I travel with my feet,
The distances are not so great
When I don't care if I am late,
I see the sights and make good friends
And walk until my journey ends.

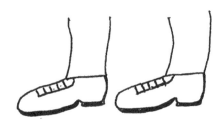

Halloween

The night darkens
And creatures of all colors
Sizes and shapes emerge,
New species never ever seen,
Except at Halloween.

All these creatures eat
Only what is sweet,
Candy, gum, and sugar corn
Is what they eat,
Their cries ring out in the night,
"Trick or treat!"

I caught one ghostlike creature
Early on that night,
It appeared upon my doorstep
And gave me quite a fright.

I picked it up and tickled it,
It laughed a laugh of joy,
Then magically it changed itself
Into a little boy.

So I'm no longer frightened
By creatures fierce and mean,
I simply smile and say to them…
"Happy Halloween!"

Counting Sheep

When I couldn't fall asleep,
I was told to count some sheep,
I closed my eyes and counted four,
But that woke me up even more,
Then I tried to count to ten,
The sheep were in my mind again.

Soon sleep came rushing to my head,
I dreamt that sheep were in my bed,
I liked the warmth of fuzzy wool,
To sleep with sheep was really cool.

The sheep were gone when I awoke,
I thought the whole thing was a joke,
But then I found some woolly hair,
I guess the sheep were really there.

So when I sleep I count to ten.
And hope the sheep come back again.

Fly Thoughts

A little fly landed nearby,
It cleaned its little wing,
It rubbed its legs together
And seemed pleased with everything.

When it saw that I was there,
It quickly flew away,
It landed on the ceiling
And was upside down that way.

I stared at it,
It stared at me,
But not a word was said,
And both of us would wonder
What was in the other's head.

The fly was thinking,
Will he smash me?
Will he try to kill?
But I was thinking,
How can a fly be standing
Upside down and be so still?

The fly decided not to wait
To see what I would do,
It dropped quickly from the ceiling
And flew far out of view.

The lesson that this taught me
Is that we can't always tell
What someone else is thinking,
Though we think we know quite well.

So when we deal with others,
It's important that we try
To think the thoughts that they think
And to ask the reasons why.

Need

Sometimes I think it's funny
That folks think it's great
To have lots of money.

Is it good to have wealth?
Is it bad to be poor?

If I have what I need,
Do I need any more?

The Beautiful Beast

I've heard of Beauty and the Beast,
It gave me quite a fright,
The Beast was very ugly,
And he howled and screamed all night.

But Beauty tamed the savage Beast,
She soothed his evil mind,
She laughed and played
And joked with him,
'Til he became quite kind.

He stopped his fits
And laughed with her,
That now became his duty
And after all was said and done,
The Beast became a Beauty.

A Lesson in Life

A small boy in Morocco
Weaving a rug on a loom,
My family watching,
The guide's proclamation,
"See, you're lucky.
You don't have to be
Like him!"

My son: high school, college,
A career, involvements,
Success and happiness,
The young rug weaver:
Poverty, suffering
And early death.

Where is equality of opportunity
And justice?
A lesson in life,
Don't waste an opportunity
That millions of others
Will never have.

My Future

When I think about my future
I don't know what I'll be,
But if I do my best
I can make much more of me.

My Greatness

Nobody says I'm great,
So I have to tell them all
That I'm the greatest person
That anyone can recall.

Why do I boast so much,
Much more than someone should?
'Cause if I didn't praise myself,
No other person would.

But someone who is truly great
Has no need to say,
'Cause others do that job
In an enthusiastic way.

Please and Thank You

Please and thank you
Are words I like to hear,
They represent politeness
That is welcome everywhere.

But sometimes we forget
To say what is polite,
We act in a rude manner
And don't say what is right.

Then we have to be reminded
Our behavior was not proper,
When my sister says rude words,
I try my best to stop her.

Foggy

When I sleep,
I sleep like a log,
When I'm awake,
I'm in a fog.

My Family

Being in a family
Is the nicest place to be,
There's a lot of talk to share
And food and fun are always there,
Brother, Sister, Mom, and Dad,
Are the ones that make me glad.

Sometimes things don't go quite right
And there may be a family fight,
But very soon after the tears
The thought of fighting disappears.
And angry feelings we had then
Are lost in family love again.

Mother's Day

Mother's Day is here again,
It comes but once a year,
Children show their love
For mothers everywhere.

I know why Mother's Day
Is always filled with joy,
"Cause there's a mother somewhere
For every girl and boy.

So celebrate on Mother's Day
And show you really care,
Because without a mother
You would not be here.

Music

Music is a pleasant sound,
That travels everywhere,
It tickles the tympanum
As it penetrates the ear.

It travels to the brain
Where it lingers for a while,
Then it goes straight to my body
And it makes my body smile.

So if I want to feel happy
I know just what to do,
I simply hum a happy tune,
Doodle, doo, de, doo.

One Penny

A little girl dropped me
Right at her feet,
I rolled from her pocket
Right onto the street.

I lay on the sidewalk
As people walked by,
They chose to ignore me
And I think I know why.

They don't seem to know
'Though I'm just one penny,
If they pick us all up
We add up to many.

A Bearded Man

I saw a bearded man
Whose face was lost in hair,
I tried to figure out
What was hidden there.

All that I could see
Was his mouth and nose and eyes,
The face behind the beard
Could be a big surprise.

His chin could be quite small
And it may well have a dimple,
Perhaps there is a scar,
Or maybe there's a pimple.

His eyes looked right at me,
His lips gave me a smile,
He knew what I was thinking,
Was he the latest style?

The man laughed at my stare,
He raised his hand to wave,
His friendly, happy manner
Made me never want to shave.

Age and Beauty

Age and beauty go together,
That's what people say,
They say it's better to be young,
But we age every day.

As we age our wisdom grows
And we grow more mature,
We become more beautiful
Than we ever were before.

So be sure to celebrate
That you've lived another year
And keep on gaining wisdom
And have a HAPPY BIRTHDAY, dear.

Older People

Many people who are old
Seem silly in their ways,
They always seem to talk
About the good old days.

They talk about the past
And how grand it used to be,
They always try to tell us
What they've stored in memory.

To them it makes no difference
That many things are past,
Because when we get older
We want the past to last.

Noses

Noses are big,
Noses are small,
They come in all shapes,
But the best thing of all,
Is though they look different,
We know very well,
No matter their shape
Noses know how to smell.

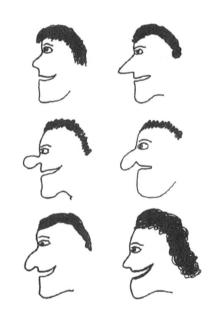

Work and Play

I do work most every day,
It's sometimes not much fun,
I try to do my best
To get lots of it done.

I grow tired every night
From work done in the day,
I go to sleep and in my dreams,
I dream that work is play.

When I awake I realize
That work is not so bad,
If I think of work as play,
I change from sad to glad.

So now when I have work to do
It doesn't bother me,
I see my work as lots of fun
And I do it cheerfully.

Jogging

Jogging is a lot of fun,
I can think while I run,
At the start I'm breathing fast,
But heavy breathing does not last.

Soon I feel like a machine,
I float along and view each scene,
My feet move quickly on the ground,
While in my mind new thoughts are found,
But the best part of the jogging hour
Is when I stop…

And take a shower.

The Grump

I am a grump.
I'm nasty and mean,
I'm the grumpiest grump
That's ever been seen.

When someone says "yes,"
I always say "no,"
I'm a negative grump
Wherever I go.

I complain about everything,
Nothing is right,
I make people miserable,
That's my delight.

Someone suggested
That I try to smile,
I think I will try,
But it may take awhile.

I'll stretch my lips
In an upward direction,
I'll practice a smile
'Til it reaches perfection.

My face looks so strange,
My lips now are curled,
My teeth are exposed,
As I smile at the world.

Hey, I never knew
That a smile feels so good,
I'm losing my grumps,
They told me I would.

My whole life is changed now,
I've learned a new style,
I'm no longer a grump,
'Cause I know how to smile.

A Teacher's Farewell

Nobody likes to say "goodbye,"
We would rather just say "hi,"
But "goodbye" means we go away,
Even though I'd rather stay.

Teaching you was lots of fun,
I'm sorry that the class is done,
We had so many special days
And learned so much so many ways.

The lessons learned should strengthen you
And help you do all that you do,
I hope what you have learned from me
Will help you be all you can be.

A Computer Nerd

A computer is my friend,
We do everything together,
I spend all my time with it,
No matter what the weather.

I play many games,
I find out many things,
I learn about the world,
About bugs and worms and kings.

I sit and punch the keys,
That's all I ever do,
My mom says I should exercise,
She says, "It's good for you."

But when I think of exercise
I lie down in my bed,
Until the thought is gone
And computers fill my head.

I never go outside,
I know it seems absurd,
Every minute of the day,
I'm a computer Nerd.

Goodbye Pacifier

I love my pacifier,
I use it day and night,
Whenever I feel sad
It makes me feel all right.

But now that I am three,
I'm old enough to say
That I'll take my pacifier
And I'll throw it away.

Goodbye, dear pacifier,
You were lots of fun,
But I don't need you anymore,
My time with you is done.

Goodbye pacifier!

More at Four

I can walk and I can talk,
I can read a children's book,
I can play computer games,
And I can even help Mom cook.

My mom says that I'm precocious,
It's a word that I don't know,
I think it means I learn things faster
Than my age should show.

I go to preschool every day,
I'm learning more and more,
Now I know most everything,
Although I'm only four.

When I'm five I'll be so smart
That everyone will say
I know this little genius
Who got smarter every day.

When I'm finally an adult,
I'll know even more,
But I guess I'll have to wait,
'Cause now I'm stuck at four.

Darkness and Light

Darkness presses heavily
On the mind, the body, and the soul,
This lasts for a moment in time,
Soon, the heavy darkness lifts
And there is light,
The cycle continues,
But eventually darkness prevails,
Even so, we are happy
Because we have seen the light…
So many times.

The Wooden Chair

The people in my house
Were very, very poor,
One day a well-dressed stranger
Came knocking at the door.

"You didn't pay the rent," he said,
"So I have to kick you out,
You don't have any money,
That's what this world's about."

The people were very sad
As they moved into the street,
They took all their belongings
And they grabbed me by my feet.

They threw me in the garbage,
Nobody seemed to care
That I was a strong and sturdy,
Old-fashioned, wooden chair.

A passing stranger noticed me
Lying in the street,
She took me to her home
And fixed my broken seat.

She treated me with kindness
And cleaned my dirt and grit,
I soon became the favorite place
For everyone to sit.

Knee Surgery

Knees are important
'Cause you need them to walk,
A mouth's important too
'Cause you need one to talk.

So I'm very happy
That your knee is in repair,
Soon you'll be walking well
And you can go most anywhere.

Be sure to exercise your knee
And keep your spirits high,
Don't be sad and gloomy
And you can bid your pain

Goodbye!

Gall Bladder Removal

A gall bladder helps
In digestion of fat,
But the good news is
You don't really need that.

Now that it's gone
You should feel very lucky,
'Cause that's one less organ
That can make you feel yukky.

Anger

Whenever I get angry
My face turns very red,
I yell out nasty words
That I never should have said.

Then anger goes away,
It disappears from sight,
It only takes a second
And then I feel all right.

Where did the anger go?
How did it go so fast?
The anger felt so strong
That I expected it to last.

When anger fills my mind
I know that it won't stay,
A smile, a laugh, a pleasant thought,
Will chase anger away.

Yoga

Yoga is very good for you,
It cheers you up when you feel blue,
You stretch your body as you pose
And the strength inside you grows.

You feel so peaceful and so calm.
The world outside can do no harm,
Your breathing becomes slow and deep,
You relax like you're asleep.

And when you wake
Your cares are gone,
You feel refreshed.
As life moves on…

My Camera

I've been to many places
And I've seen many things,
I've had many adventures
And the thrills that travel brings.

When I return from traveling
People always want to see
The photographs I've taken
Of the things that interest me.

But I don't use a camera
When I travel far away,
I take pictures with my eyes
And in my brain they stay.

Toothless

When I looked into a mirror
My mouth looked very weird,
My front teeth had fallen out,
They had simply disappeared.

But I wasn't very sad,
Losing teeth was not that scary,
'Cause I knew there'd be a visit
From the generous Tooth Fairy.

I went to sleep that night
And before I closed my eyes,
The Tooth Fairy appeared,
(It was my mother in disguise).

She gently put two dollars
Underneath my head,
One for each tooth lost
Lay hidden in my bed.

Every tooth I lost
Made my mouth look funny,
But each time I lost a tooth
I gained lots of money.

Soon new teeth appeared,
A new smile was on my face
And the Tooth Fairy took her money
To another mouth someplace.

Pills

Blue and yellow,
Pink and gray,
These are pills
I take each day.

When I was young
I had no ills,
I had no need
For any pills.

Now that I'm older
It's no surprise
That body parts fail
And illnesses arise.

Pills are now my friends,
They comfort me each day,
They keep my juices flowing
And chase the pains away.

I used to take just two a day,
I now take more than five,
Pills, pills, and more pills
Now keep me alive.

My Haircut

When my hair looks like a mop
I run right to the barber shop,
My friendly barber's always there
To cut and groom my messy hair.

He cuts each hair
With pride and skill,
He does his art
While I sit still.

I watch each hair
Float to the floor,
The hair piles up
But he cuts more.

My hair looks short
But there's no sorrow,
Hair today…
And gone tomorrow.

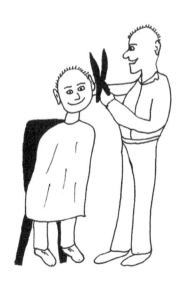

The Mirror Man

When I look into a mirror
I see that I am there,
Every detail of myself
Is extremely clear.

The Mirror Man has features
That are the same as mine,
Our funny face and droopy nose
Are of the same design.

We look so much alike
And he does all that I do,
I wonder if he thinks
The same thoughts I think too?

I tried to touch the Mirror Man
But I hit against the glass,
The mirror blocked my way
And it would not let me pass.

So I just look in the mirror
And I smile at what I see,
The Mirror Man is smiling too
'Cause he knows that he is me.

Finding Our Way

When my wife and I are lost
While driving in our car,
I stop people on the street
To ask them where we are.

My wife uses maps
To find out information,
She never asks a passerby
To tell us our location.

Now our problem is resolved
And we no longer have to guess
Where we are or where we're going,
'Cause we bought a GPS.

My GPS is named Carla,
She's now part of my life,
She is wise and thoughtful
And is like a second wife.

Now when I am driving
Two voices scream at me,
My wife yells words of warning,
Carla tells me where to be.

Myself

Once in awhile
When I have a bad day,
I want to escape
to a land far away.

But I can't really escape,
That's something I know,
'Cause I take myself with me
Wherever I go.

So I have to like me,
And like what I do,
Then I can feel happy
And live life better too.

A Lifetime

When I was a little baby
My screams made lots of noise,
I hugged my little teddy
And I played with many toys.

Then as I grew older
And became a little boy,
A small laptop computer
Became my favorite toy.

Adulthood was my favorite time,
I had a job and money,
I had a wife and children,
And I had a dog named Honey.

Old age happened suddenly,
Time was quick to disappear,
Before I knew what happened,
The Golden Years were here.

When I look into a mirror
And I see my wrinkled face,
I think of past experiences
That old age can't erase.

I'm not sorry to be old
For I've seen many things,
My memories prepare me
For what the future brings.

Arithmetic

I was feeling very sad
'Cause I had never learned to add,
I also could not multiply,
Arithmetic had passed me by,
Division was a mystery,
And fractions brought me misery.

I could not stand it anymore,
So I went to the computer store,
The store clerk listened to my plea,
He said he had something for me,
He said that I could pay him later
For a solar calculator.

Now I'm happy as can be,
The calculator adds and subtracts for me,
I have no need to use my head,
I press calculator keys instead.

Now I'll never make mistakes…
Until the calculator breaks.

The Lonely Boy

The little boy was lonely,
He sat and watched TV,
I asked if he liked poetry
But he didn't answer me.

I sat down next to him
And I read poems from my book,
At first he seemed suspicious,
Soon he had a smiling look.

I gave him a copy of the book
To be read by his mom or dad,
"My mom and dad broke up," he said.
The boy seemed very sad.

I read him many poems
And he listened eagerly,
He was thinking about life
And the fun that it could be.

It made me feel so good
When he laughed so happily,
I had added to his life
The joy of poetry.

Family Visits

When I visit relatives
We always hug and kiss,
That's a part of family life
That I would like to miss.

But my mom tells me to do it,
So that's what I will do,
I'll kiss everyone in sight,
Uncles, aunts, and cousins too.

I'll kiss my way into the house,
That's what visits are about
And when I leave I'll say goodbye.
And kiss my pathway out.

The Bully

They call me a bully,
I'm disliked by all,
I push kids around
And I laugh as they fall.

Some kids are friendly
And some kids are not,
I bully them all.
No matter what.

Here comes someone
Who is bigger than me,
He looks like a bully,
But he's nice as can be.

He relates well to others,
His friendliness shows,
Everyone likes him
Wherever he goes.

I'm probably foolish
To act as I do,
If I wasn't a bully
I'd have friends too.

Being Alone

I sat alone one day
And watched the people walking,
They had iPods in their ears,
Or were on their cell phones, talking.

I thought how nice it was
To be sitting all alone
And watch nature all around me
And not be on the phone.

A squirrel darted by,
And I watched a honeybee,
I saw flowers show their colors
And green leaves dressed up the tree.

It was a cloudy day.
But the temperature was warm,
I felt the breeze and wondered
If there'd be a thunderstorm.

I sat there all alone
While I heard their cell phones ringing,
They had iPods in their ears.
While I heard robins singing.

The Cookie Man

I am the Cookie Man,
I eat as many as I can,
There never is an end,
Every cookie is my friend.

Chocolate and vanilla too,
It makes no difference
Which I chew,

When I come near
They run away,
'Cause I will eat them
If they stay.

The Door of Life

The door opens,
Life begins,
Much happiness,
Moments of glory,
Triumphs and defeats,
Feelings of love,
Seconds of sadness,
Worries that wax and wane,
Promises made and broken,
Words never spoken,
Memories that fade,
Suddenly…
The door slams shut…
Was it just the wind?

Owasco Marina

In my super motorboat
I explored Owasco Lake,
The boat was strong and sturdy,
I thought no part could break.

Then one day I turned the key
To make the engine run,
No sound was heard and I could tell
My boat's good days were done.

But then from somewhere came a call,
"We can take care of that."
I turned my head and there he was,
With a wet suit and a hat.

The handsome stranger spoke to me
And said what he could do,
"I'll take the boat to my marina
And make it almost new."

He fixed the boat in just a day,
Now it's as good as new,
Everything works perfectly,
There's nothing more to do.

Owasco Marina is the place
To fix every kind of boat,
Nice people and good service too
Will keep your boat afloat.

The Skaneateles Festival

Strolling near the lake,
Doing lots of shopping,
Eating tasty meals
And desserts with chocolate topping.

Then the night came on,
People gathered on the grass,
Behind a lovely house.
Where some magic hours would pass.

The children sat on blankets,
The adults sat on chairs,
But no matter where we sat,
Music filled our ears.

The flute sounded its magic
And the clarinet did too,
The violins played softly
And the golden trumpets blew.

Stars above were dancing.
The moon lit up the sky,
The music made us dream
About happy days gone by.

We flew to wondrous places,
The music was our wing,
We had warm and pleasant feelings
That each melody would bring.

This was something not to miss,
That night at Skaneateles.

The Mountain Bus

The bus climbed up the mountain,
The road was very steep,
I wondered what would happen
If the driver fell asleep.

The trip was very dangerous
As we headed toward the top,
One slip of the wheel
And we'd have a mighty drop.

When we reached the top
After such a scare,
It was a great surprise
To find other buses there.

Nothing

I have many things
That I love and treasure,
Just knowing that I have them
Gives me lots of pleasure.

If I gave everything away
And had only nothing left,
Then I wouldn't have to worry
About any kind of theft.

Having nothing would be great,
There'd be nothing everywhere,
Wherever I would go,
Nothing would be there.

It would be very lonely
When I walk down the street,
Since nothing would be there,
There'd be nobody to meet.

When I write a poem
There'll be nothing to say,
But I'll just keep on writing
Until something comes my way.

N
O
T
H
I
N
G

FOOD

Grapes

I bought a bunch of grapes,
The price was very low,
I wondered how they tasted,
There was one way I could know.

I put one in my mouth,
Its skin was green and slick,
I crunched it with my teeth,
And chewed it up real quick.

A burst of flavor filled my mouth,
The taste was really good,
I liked the grapes so well
That I ate more than I should.

So now my stomach's full,
I can't eat any more,
If you mention grapes to me,
I'll throw up on the floor.

Pizza

I have a special treat for you,
A pizza that is truly new,
Use tomato paste and cheese
And whatever else you please.

Add some nuts and macaroni,
Then throw in some beef baloney,
Sprinkle it with lots of candy,
Use whatever else is handy.

Pickles are a tasty treat,
They make the pizza good to eat,
Then add some tangerines
And cover them with chocolate beans.

Then soak it all in sweetened flour
And bake the mix for just an hour,
When the pizza's finally done,
Give a piece to everyone.

Eating this will make them smile
And they'll be in the bathroom for a while.

Chips

Potato chips are great to eat,
They are now my favorite treat,
I like the salty taste
And I like the way they crunch,
I eat them as a snack
And I eat them with my lunch.

I try not to eat too many,
I really try my best,
But after I eat one,
I must eat all the rest.

Mom hides the potato chips
On a high shelf in the hall,
I know the secret hiding place
But I am not that tall.

So I can't reach the chips
And the best that I can do,
Is dream I eat potato chips
And hope my dream comes true.

Special Sandwich

I start with toasted bread,
And then I add some meat,
Ham, turkey, and salami
Are what I like to eat.

Then I put on lettuce
And add a slice of cheese,
This sandwich seems so good.
But it needs much more please.

So I add a bit of honey,
And peanut butter too,
With mayonnaise and mustard,
The sandwich tastes like glue.

But it's a special sandwich
That shouldn't go to waste,
So chew and swallow quickly
To avoid its special taste.

Too Fat

I ate a lot of food
And I became too fat,
I grew too big all over,
Especially where I sat.

I can't imagine how
I grew fatter than a cow,
So one day I decided
To lose a lot of weight,
I went on a strict diet
And I started to feel great.

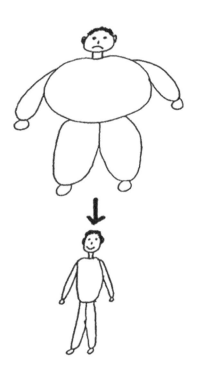

I exercised each day
And much to my surprise,
I lost a lot of pounds
And became a smaller size.

If you get fat like I did
And want to lose weight too,
Exercise and eating less
Can do the job for you.

Fried Foods

Fried foods are not good for you,
They make you grow too fat,
They block up all your arteries,
You get heart attacks from that.

So be sure to watch your diet,
Eat foods that are good for you,
Then you'll live a long and healthy life
And you'll be skinny too.

Sweet Dreams

When I go to sleep at night
I never seem to know
Where my dreams will take me
And what wonders they will show.

Last night I was in candy land,
The first time I've been there,
Lollipops and candy bars
Could be found everywhere.

Chocolate fudge and Tootsie Rolls,
Smarties, Skittles too,
Any candy you could want
Was there for me and you.

I ate a Gummi Teddy Bear
And licked a lollipop,
I ate and ate and ate and ate,
I couldn't seem to stop.

My stomach got so full
That I started to feel sick,
But just then I awoke,
And I woke up very quick.

My stomach pain was gone,
No candy was in sight,
The happy trip to candy land
Had passed by in the night.

But I enjoyed that dream,
It was really fun,
I hope that tomorrow's sleep
Will bring another one.

The Growling Stomach

I hear my stomach growl,
It sounds just like a bear,
I cannot figure out
What is happening there.

I eat a bit of food.
This makes the growling stop,
The animal in my stomach.
Must like the food a lot.

So whenever in my stomach
It sounds like there's a riot,
I simply eat a bagel
And it keeps the animal quiet.

Ice Is Nice

My drink was warm, it tasted bad,
The worst drink that I've ever had,
Then I had some good advice,
A friend told me to add some ice.

So I put ice cubes in my drink,
They floated there and did not sink,
I watched the ice cubes disappear,
They went away, I know not where.

Soon the cubes were fully gone,
But their coldness lingered on,
Now the drink was really good,
It tasted like a good drink should.

The ice cubes never became old,
They disappeared, but left the cold,
I thanked my friend for good advice,
'Cause now I know that ice is nice.

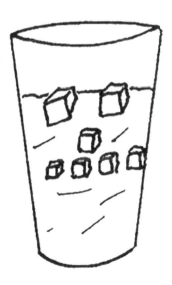

Salt

Glistening crystals
Dissolving rapidly,
Vanishing from sight,
Soon invisible,
But flavorful,
Evaporation of clear liquid
Brings white crystals back again,
We stare in amazement and behold
Another chance at life.

Sharing a Bagel

We both wanted a bagel,
But there was only one,
I thought of how to share it
And it was lots of fun.

I said we should pretend
That the bagel was a roll,
I tore it right in half
And gave my friend the hole.

LOVE AND CARING

What Love Means

One day while walking down the street
A little girl I did meet,
She said that she wanted to find
How the word *love* might be defined.

The meaning was inside my head
And I was pleased with what I said,
"Love is when I want to do
Less for me, and more for you."

My Teddy

I love my little teddy bear,
He is my favorite friend,
I go to sleep with him each night,
On that you can depend.

Sometimes, I awaken him
In the middle of the night,
I tell him funny stories
And I giggle with delight.

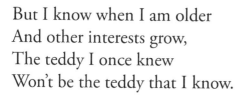

I love my little teddy bear,
I take him every place,
He feels so warm and cuddly
When I hug him to my face.

But I know when I am older
And other interests grow,
The teddy I once knew
Won't be the teddy that I know.

Now he is so dear to me,
But when I'm more mature,
The teddy of my childhood
Will be gone forevermore.

But no matter what my age.
And no matter where I'll be
I'll always have my teddy
As a happy memory.

Good night, teddy…
Wherever you are.

My Secret Friend

When I go to sleep each night
I meet a secret friend,
I tell it all my cares
As the day comes to an end.

I press my cheek against it
And I hold it very tight,
I whisper that "I love you,"
And then turn out the light.

I sleep a peaceful sleep
And feel so warm and snug,
All because my "blankie"
Gives me a great big hug.

The Tree

A tree that stands so straight and high
Spreads its branches toward the sky,
The branches are a lovely sight,
The leaves on them are green and bright.

The tree that stands above the ground
Has hidden roots that can be found,
Below the earth we cannot see
The roots that help support the tree.

They give it strength and water too,
We cannot see all that they do
And just as roots support the tree,
My family gives support to me.

My Secret

I had a little secret
Hidden in my mind,
It stayed inside my head
And was very hard to find.

One day my little secret
Caused a bit of pain,
As it squeezed out of my head
And departed from my brain.

It reached my lips
And leaped outside
Right into the air,
My little secret now was out
For everyone to hear.

What was this little secret
Now every person knew?
That precious little secret was that

I

LOVE

U

Love and Laugh

I try to laugh my way through life
But when I'm feeling sad,
I have a way to smile again
And change the sad to glad.

Making joy return
Is an easy thing to do,
I simply fill my mind
With loving thoughts of you.

When you are in my mind
You fill up all the space,
Sad thoughts cannot fit
And they go some other place.

Then I'm happy once again,
It happens very fast,
Just the thought that I love you
Puts sadness in the past…

And makes my laughter last.

Darkness, Light, and Love

The room was dark,
There was no light,
Yet this darkness
Was not night.

My thoughts were sad,
They made life dark,
My life was empty,
There was no spark.

Suddenly the room lit up,
Happiness had come,
The brilliance was amazing
And I knew where it was from.

She lit up the room,
Her beauty was so bright,
Her laugh made me so happy
It removed the black of night.

So whenever darkness comes
I think of my dear one
And then the light bulbs glow
And all of life is fun.

Booky and Cooky

Booky Tooky once met Cooky,
They made a handsome pair,
Booky Tooky married Cooky
And after just a year,
Booky Tooky had a baby,
A cuddly little boy,
They had to find a name for him,
A name he would enjoy,
Finally, they chose a name,
They named him after Booky,
The baby's name that Booky chose
Was Booky Tooky Shnooky.

A Kinder, Better Place

One day I saw an old man
Walking down the street,
He had a cane and limped along
And rags were on his feet.

I stopped to ask him why
His feet appeared so funny,
He answered me and said,
"Because I have no money."

"I can help," I said,
"For I have hidden treasure,
I can buy some shoes for you,
It will be my pleasure."

The old man seemed surprised and said,
"But why should you help me?
I'm just a poor old man
With no shoes, as you can see?"

"That's why I want to help you,
When I see someone poor,
I think about my own wealth
And that I have so much more."

"So I want to share my wealth
With those who are in need,
It makes me feel so good
To do a thoughtful deed."

I wish that others wanted
To help the human race,
If that were true the world
Would be a kinder, better place.

Sharing Wealth

If I had lots of money,
I'd travel far and near,
I'd visit Greece and Spain,
I'd go most everywhere.

In every place I'd stay awhile
And I would live in wealthy style,
I'd buy the finest clothes and such
And I would never lack for much.

But would it make me feel so good.
To have more than one person should?
The world has many mouths to feed
And I'll have much more than I need.

So I'll stop spending more and more,
I'll give my money to the poor
And though my money would depart,
My wealth would be within my heart.

Two Old Horses

Two old horses in the field,
Both of them were white,
They rubbed against each other
And whinnied in delight.

They shared the field together,
They had lots of grass and space,
They were happy older horses
Who lived at their own pace.

I went to see them yesterday
And much to my surprise
Only one white horse was there,
I could not believe my eyes.

"What happened to your friend?" I asked,
"Where did your partner go?"
The old horse stared at me,
She seemed to think I'd know

That her partner left this world,
That he left her all alone,
That her happiness had gone,
That her world had turned to stone.

But she was brave and strong,
She overcame her sadness,
She thought about the pleasant past
And sadness turned to gladness.

The happy memories of him
Brought her joy and laughter
And even though she missed him.
She lived happily ever after.

Three Horse Friends

The old white horse
Who lost her mate
Stood bravely in the field,
She lived with pleasant memories
That thoughts of him revealed.

When I drove by the other day
I was pleased to see
Two brown horses in the field,
To make the total three.

They say that three's a crowd,
But they were a lovely sight,
Three horse friends in the meadow,
Together day and night.

Organic Love

I love you with all my heart,
My kidneys love you too,
My lungs are crazy 'bout you,
They love everything you do.

I love you so madly
That sometimes I will shiver,
Every organ starts to shake,
Especially my liver.

My intestine fills with gas,
My stomach starts to churn,
My muscles start contracting.
My appendix starts to burn,

My heart beats very rapidly
And keeps the bloodstream flowing,
All my organs are excited
As my love for you keeps growing.

Sharing

I visited the zoo one day
And saw a funny sight,
Two elephants were side by side
And almost had a fight.

One elephant was eating hay,
The other wanted it,
The first one took the hay away
And would not share a bit.

People can be selfish too
And never want to share,
Even if they have enough
They don't seem to care.

We hope that they will change.
But that's very hard to do,
Selfish people do exist.
But don't let one be you.

Blue Is You

Your hair is blue
Your face is too
I have no clue
Why all of you
Is colored blue.

I know it's true
That blue is you
From every view
There's only blue.

What I must do
To make you new
Is color your head
And make it red.

Color me Blue

Color me Red

Happiness and Sadness

Life has happy days,
But there are sad ones too,
Some days are filled with laughter
And other days are blue.

There are always days
When nothing goes quite right,
We feel alone and sad
And there is no joy in sight.

The way to handle sad days
Is to expect that they will be,
There will be happy days
And there'll be days of misery.

Whenever sad things happen
Keep in mind that they won't stay,
Happy times will come again
And brighten up your day.

How They Met

She splashed some water on my face,
To her it was a joke,
I laughed and choked and coughed
And then she finally spoke.

"What is your name?" she asked me
And "What job do you do?"
"I see you like to swim.
That's something I like too."

We talked and laughed together
Until we knew each other well,
Friendship changed to love,
As everyone could tell.

Now it's many years ago
That we met there in the water,
We've been together ever since
And have two sons and a daughter.

Just Plain Love

Love is something wonderful,
It makes me feel so good,
It helps me live my life
Like no other feeling could.

No matter where I go
You are always there,
You're built into my mind,
So when you're far, you're near.

You are a part of me
That will stay forevermore,
No matter what I do
It's you that I adore.

My love gives me the strength
To survive when things go wrong,
Just the thought of you
Makes my mind and body strong.

So I never am alone.
Since my love will always be,
Whenever troubles come
You'll be there to comfort me.

My Baby Sister

A baby was born,
It was a new sister,
She cried very loud,
But she stopped
When I kissed her.

When she was a baby
She made lots of noise,
I didn't like her
When she played with my toys.

I screamed at my sister
And she ran away,
As small little children
We fought every day.

My mom yelled at me
To be friendly and nice,
But I still teased my sister,
Despite Mom's advice.

But when we grew older
The fights came to an end,
My once baby sister
Is now my best friend.

Aging

We get older every day,
There's not much we can do,
The years fly by too quickly
And youth fades out of view.

In younger days an illness
Would be someone else's thing,
Now illness greets old age
And we take pills for everything.

Pains are not uncommon,
Arms and legs both ache,
Walking becomes difficult
And bones can split and break.

We lose much of our abilities,
But our emotions stay,
We still can love and laugh,
And that will never go away.

To Pat on Our 50th Anniversary

We've been married 50 years
And I am pleased to say,
That the love that we have shared
Grows stronger every day.

We've shared so many things
And we've had so much fun,
Our special traits are different
But in spirit we are one.

Love and friendship last forever,
They never fade away,
We walk and talk together
And we laugh at life each day.

50 years have passed.
They went by very fast,
But our love stays young
And forever it will last.

Happy 50th Anniversary!

Marvin

To Pat on Our 52nd Anniversary

52 is special,
It's one more than 51,
It's one less than 53
And it's the only one.

We'll celebrate 52
'Cause that's how many years
That we have been together
And shared each other's cares.

Living life together,
Laughing every day,
Making precious memories
That time can't take away.

Your ways of life are wonderful.
Your beauty makes you glow,
With your happy, caring manner,
You're the very best I know.

So, Happy Anniversary,
It's number 52,
I've been very lucky
To have shared my life with you.

Happy 52nd Anniversary!

Marvin

To Pat on Our 55th Anniversary

55 is special,
It's one more than 54,
It's one less than 56
And it has never been before.

We'll celebrate 55,
'Cause that's how many years
That we have been together
And shared each other's cares.

Living life together,
Laughing every day,
Making precious memories
That time can't take away.

Your ways of life are wonderful.
Your beauty makes you glow,
With your happy, caring manner.
You're the very best I know.

So, Happy Anniversary,
It's number 55,
As long as time exists,
Our love will stay alive.

Happy 55th Anniversary!

Marvin

Pat   Marvin

Death of a Loved One

Sparkling visions danced,
They filled my heart with joy,
Everything was happy
When I was just a boy.

Then I grew much older,
The time went by so fast,
I married and we had children,
My younger days were past.

I had many happy years
With my wife here at my side,
She was my shining angel,
No man had such a bride.

We loved and laughed together,
The joy went on and on,
Then illness struck her down
And my precious wife was gone.

It's hard to be alone,
It all seems so unreal,
No person can imagine
The emptiness I feel.

Yet life must still be lived
And even though I'm sad,
I will always treasure
The happy days we had.

BEASTS, BUGS, PLANTS, AND NATURE

The Not-Real Crocodile

My head has tiny feathers,
I also have small wings,
My mouth has purple teeth,
My legs are twisted things.

I eat everything in sight,
Bananas, bugs, and snakes,
I drink milk and lemonade,
And I love chocolate cakes.

I used to frighten people
But my outside isn't me,
Inside I am beautiful,
Now that's what people see.

'Though I look very strange
I always do good deeds,
I try in every way to help
People who have needs.

When I meet people in the street
They greet me with a smile,
'Cause they are pleased to know
A friendly, not-real crocodile.

My Dog Max

I have a dog named Max,
He's big and has brown hair,
He follows me around
When I go anywhere.

He always wants to play
With his favorite squeaky toy,
I just toss it in the air
And yell, "Go get it, boy!"

I had a sandwich on my plate,
It was toasted ham and cheese,
He ate it from the table
Without even saying please.

Wherever my feet walk
Max is in the way,
No matter what I'm doing
He always wants to play.

When I take Max outside
I take along a scoop,
'Cause I know that I will have to
Clean up all his poop.

Max barks at every person
When he wants to say hello,
He tries to lick your face
Because he likes you so.

Max loves everyone
And he never tries to bite,
He wags his tail with joy
When people are in sight.

Whenever I feel tired
I know how to relax,
I close my eyes and think
About my friendly dog…
Named Max.

Goodbye Max

Max grew old and ill
And he finally passed away,
My dog was gone forever,
It was a sad, sad day.

I cried myself to sleep,
There was no end to sorrow,
My life was full of sadness,
Max would not be here tomorrow.

I wondered about life
And why it has to end,
Why did Max have to die
When he was my best friend?

'Cause it's a rule of nature
That all living things must die,
All life lasts just a moment
And then must say goodbye.

But Max had a happy life,
His time on earth was good,
We shared many happy moments
And he lived life as best he could.

Although I'm very sad
'Cause he's no longer here,
My love for him stays strong
And Max will never disappear.

Gone Fishing

Grandpa likes to fish,
He has a rod and reel,
He starts out every morning
To catch his evening meal.

I know that he is out there
Trying to catch me,
He looks in many places
But does not know where I'll be.

I avoid his fishing line,
I swim around his hook,

As long as I am careful
It won't be me he'll cook.

Grandpa meets his friends
And he tells everyone
That he didn't catch a fish
But he had lots of fun.

Grandpa and the fish
Were happy on that day,
Grandpa had his fun
And the fish all got away.

The Laughing Kookaburra

The kookaburra is a bird
That laughs the whole day through,
It always seems so happy,
There are no days when it's blue.

It laughs when there is joy,
It laughs when there is pain,
It laughs when there is sunshine,
It laughs when there is rain.

Laughter chases cares away
No matter where you'll be,
So be sure to keep on laughing,
Ha, Ha, Ha and He, He, He.

This and That

Skinny
cat
named
PAT
sat
on
Mat
ate
Rat
Got
Fat

DRAT!

The Spider

The spider made its web,
It was a pretty sight,
The silky threads were hard to see.
Especially at night.

I flew right toward my home
That was behind the tree,
I didn't see the spider's web
Until it had trapped me.

I hit against the threads
And my body stuck right there,
I struggled to get free
But the web seemed everywhere.

My struggle gave the signal
And then out came the spider
And before I knew what happened
I ended up inside her.

The Worm

It was on the sidewalk,
A curled figure,
It was all alone,
No other worms in sight,
How did it live?
How did it die?
Was it missed by its family?
Did it have a happy life?
There were no answers,
It was now only
A curled figure
On the sidewalk.

Crows

Early in the evening
I looked up at the sky
And saw hundreds of crows
Quickly flying by.

Before the end of evening
They settled on a tree,
They looked like blackened leaves
That seemed to stare at me.

I wanted to find out
What each crow had to say,
But they cackled to each other
In a most peculiar way.

'Though their language was a secret,
The noise they made was loud,
The sight and noise of crows
Made people form a crowd.

While people watched below
I climbed into the tree,
I sat upon a branch
And the crows surrounded me.

I stayed up there all night,
Then early the next day,
The crows awakened me.
And we all flew away.

The Firefly

Night was almost here,
It was becoming dark,
I stared into the blackness
And saw a tiny spark.

I cupped my hand around the spark
And caught the flashing bug,
I put it in a tiny jar
To keep it warm and snug.

The firefly lit its tail,
It wanted to get out,
But there was no escape,
Of that there was no doubt.

Then I started to feel sorry
For this lonely, sparkling star,
The bug belonged in nature
And not in this glass jar.

I opened up the jar
So the firefly could flee,
It flashed its light in gratitude
And joined its family.

Help Free Me

I hit against the silky threads
And I couldn't get away,
My struggles did no good,
It was not my lucky day.

Then a face appeared,
She had a friendly smile,
She stared at me with interest
And studied me awhile.

Meanwhile I had lost all hope
And thought I'd soon be dead,
When suddenly from nowhere
A hand brushed past my head.

It broke the web that held me.
Now I was filled with glee,
The friendly little girl
Just now had made me free.

So when someone is in trouble
And no one seems to care,
I make a special effort
To be sure my help is there.

The Caterpillar

I saw a fuzzy caterpillar
Crawling on the ground,
It was all alone,
No others were around.

It moved in one direction,
It seemed to have no fear,
I touched it with a leaf,
But it didn't seem to care.

The caterpillar knew
That it was on its way
To some special place,
But where, I cannot say.

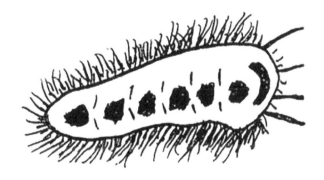

The Ant

Moving quickly,
Erratic, but purposeful,
Back toward the nest,
A bit of food is in my mouth,
Friends and family await me,
I am strong and sturdy,
Life is good,
A sudden shadow,
Huge beyond belief,.
Descending with force,
A crunching sound…
That I never heard.

The Last Leaf to Drop

I was young and green,
My stem was very strong,
I was part of an oak tree
To which other leaves belong.

I used water every day
And took in CO_2,
I made sugar in the sun,
Like all the green plants do.

The summer passed,
Then came the Fall,
That's when I saw
A change for all.

Leaves were changing colors,
Green was no longer there,
Many leaves fell from the tree
Until the tree was almost bare.

I felt the Autumn breeze
And thought about the past,
I had many happy memories
That made me want to last.

But my happy life was over,
It was time to leave the tree,
The others were all gone,
The last leaf to drop was

Tomatoes*

Tomatoes are my favorite food,
They're the crop my father grows,
They make me feel so healthy
From my head right to-ma-toes.

---

* This poem was the winner of the Post-Standard Tomatofest Poetry Contest in Auburn, New York, 2008

Living Plants

How do plants know the hour
When it's time to grow a flower?
Why do plants bend toward the light?
How can they tell the day from night?

We know some of the answers
But we don't know them very well,
When we study plants
There's much more to tell.

We may think plants are lifeless
When we put them on display,
'Though plants don't look like people,
They're alive in every way.

Floating Seeds

The little seeds are all around,
They float in windy air,
They all have fibrous feathers
That can fly them anywhere.

Most of the seeds will perish,
They'll land where they can't grow,
But some will land in fertile soil
And that will start the show.

Then the miracle of life
Will unleash its powers
And the little floating seeds
Will grow into plants
With lovely flowers.

The Yellow Day Lily

The yellow flower was beautiful,
It sparkled in the sun,
I put it in a vase
To be seen by everyone.

I told my wife the flower
Was as beautiful as she,
They both had special features
That brought happiness to me.

The next day the flower was gone,
It lay upon the floor,
It now was shrunken orange
And its yellow was no more.

It was here for just an instant,
But then it went away,
I wish this lovely lily
Could have stayed
    just
       one
          more
            day.

Deer Everywhere

The deer destroyed my garden,
They ate everything in sight,
I chased them in the daytime
But they came again at night.

There were so many deer
And they ate the plants I grow,
I wondered where they lived,
There was one way I could know.

I followed one deer home
As it left my garden patch,
It ran into the forest
And was very hard to catch.

Then I saw it stop
behind an old oak tree,
I was pleased to see
That it had a family.

When I plant my garden next year,
There'll be food for all the deer.
Then I'm sure they'll breed
And we'll have more deer…
Everywhere.

A Flower and Frost

The air was cold,
There was a breeze,
There was a danger
Flowers would freeze.

A red tulip could be seen,
Its stem was long and straight,
It stretched up toward the sky
And was concerned about its fate.

The flower stood up tall
As it fought the bitter frost,
It did everything it could
To stay alive at any cost.

The next day the sun shone brightly
And the frost melted away,
The tulip spread its petals,
This was a happy day.

The frost was gone for summer,
The air no longer would be colder,
Now the tulip could experience
The joys of growing older.

A Green Plant

I wish I were a green plant,
I would stand tall every day,
I would dance in pleasant breezes
And have lots of fun that way.

I would make pretty flowers
And spread my seeds around,
I would soak in happy showers
And grow roots underground.

But the best thing I would do,
I would do just in the sun,
I'd do photosynthesis
And make food for everyone.

The Lonely Flower

The beautiful flower was all by itself,
Its colors were yellow and white,
It sparkled in the sunshine.
It was truly a glorious sight.

But this flower was all alone
There were no others near,
The beautiful little flower
Had loneliness to fear.

Then one day some seeds
Dropped onto the ground,
They soon grew into plants
And more flowers could be found.

So now our flower is happy,
It has new pretty friends,
Oneness grew to manyness,
That's how our story ends.

The Fallen Leaf

I saw a yellow leaf
Hanging on a tree,
The leaf remembers well
How green it used to be.

The wind blows briskly
And the leaf begins to drop,
It joins other yellow leaves
Gently falling from the top.

The yellow leaf seems sad
As it softly hits the ground,
It wants to find its youth,
But no greenness can be found.

The yellow leaf knows well
That it has a sorry fate,
It will disappear,
While the naked tree will wait
Until the breath of Springtime
Once again is here.

Then tiny buds will blossom
And new green leaves will appear.

Rainbow

The colors of a rainbow
Seem so bright and clear,
Red and yellow, green and blue
Are curved up in the air.

When the rain departs
And clouds move out of sight,
The colors of the rainbow
Mix together and look white.

When clouds return again
And raindrops start to fall,
The colors of the rainbow
Can again be seen by all.

Birds, Cats, and Squirrels

I have a birdhouse in my yard,
I watch it every day,
The birds fly in and eat the seeds
And then they fly away.

Before the birds go near the seeds
They always look around,
They seem to want to see
If danger can be found.

One day a cat was in my yard
The birds showed lots of fear,
They quickly flew away
'Cause they knew the cat was there.

When squirrels came to eat the
    seeds
The birds did not seem scared,
They simply ate their tasty lunch
And birds and squirrels shared.

How can the birds tell who's who?
How can the birds decide
Whether they should eat the seeds,
Or fly away and hide?

I don't know the answer
And I can't really say
If a bird knows what it's doing
When it behaves that way.

Birds know that squirrels are not
    cats
And birds do not show fear,
Can it be that birds can think
And know when danger's near?

Snow

Do you know about snow?
It falls from the sky, you know,
It covers everything in sight,
A blanket white as white is white,
It surely is a pretty sight.

A fluffy pillow in the sky
Spills its feathers from on high
And all the flakes come floating down
And cover all that's in our town.

I love to watch the snowflakes fall,
I'd like to try to catch them all
And every flake is special too,
Its shape is something that's brand-new.

I treasure every one of them,
'Cause each will never be again,
Each melts into a spot of wet
That disappears.
With no regret.

Ducks

The ducks went swimming by,
They looked so calm and slow,
But their feet were moving quickly
As they paddled from below.

They flew in a formation,
Each duck knew where to be,
The ducks' complex behavior
Seemed a mystery to me.

They swam in icy water
But they did not seem to care,
They seemed so warm and cozy
As they swam from here somewhere.

How did they fly that way?
And how did they keep warm?
What did they eat for food?
How did ducks survive a storm?

Then suddenly one duck
Flew into the sky.
The other ducks soon followed,
'Til all were flying high.

I wondered where they went?
And will the ducks come back?
I asked one duck these questions
And his answer was:
        QUACK!
        QUACK!

A Lonely Bird

Little bird upon the window sill,
Why do you sit so very still?
While other birds are on the wing,
You sit alone and do not sing,
When you look and see me near,
You do not flee and show no fear.

You do not either feed nor drink,
I wonder what your mind does think?
Did you lose a lovely mate?
Or are you thinking of your fate?
Maybe you don't think at all
But simply follow nature's call.

I'll give you some enriching grain,
That should bring you joy again,
But when I approach the place you stay,
You chirp at me
       And
         Fly
           Away.

Listen to Nature

I love the sounds of nature,
A bird, a brook, a tree,
Everything in nature
Speaks special things to me.

Nature says birds are happy
And trees are happy too,
The brook that babbles onward
Has little else to do.

But humans often mess things up
And destroy the natural state,
Sometimes they are sorry
But sorrow comes too late.

Humans have to listen
To what nature has to say,
Otherwise their actions
May make nature fade away.

Life Is Everywhere

I overturned a rock
And saw a wondrous sight,
Creatures of all sorts
Came out into the light.

A ladybug, a sowbug,
A millipede and some ants,
I sat down on the ground
And the ants crawled up my pants.

All these creatures hustled,
There was no time to spare,
They looked for food and water
And scrambled everywhere.

I put the rock back in its place
And the creatures disappeared,
Although I had disturbed them,
They did not seem to be scared.

The lesson that I learned
Is that life is all around
And if you don't believe me.
Lift a rock up from the ground.

Super Zillions

How much life is on the earth?
That's very hard to know,
We see life on earth's surface
And there's also life below.

I tried to count all living things
But there are too many creatures,
Each one of every group
Has its own special features.

I counted things that fly
And I counted things that crawl,
I counted things that swim,
But I couldn't count them all.

My counting had no ending,
Life was beyond the trillions,
I had to make new numbers
So I made up—**SUPER ZILLIONS**.

The Active Rock

I found a rock the other day,
It was round and hard and gray,
I picked it up from where it lay
And thought what it could do today.

It could be a display,
It could make some papers stay,
It could block a passageway,
It could hide some ants at play.

I gave the rock a big "Hooray,"
And then...
I threw the rock away.

To Step or Not to Step

The ant seemed very happy
Until I dug into the ground,
Then the ant climbed out
And wandered all around.

It seemed a bit bewildered
And did not know what to do,
It ran right toward my foot
And went underneath my shoe.

That posed a major problem
I had to solve real fast,
Should I step down with my shoe?
Or should I allow the ant to last?

Please help me to decide
While the ant is still in view,
To step or not to step?
What do you think I should do?

You Can Write Poems Too

Eggs

eggs ⓞ ⓞ ⓞ ⓞ ⓞ
eggs are very pretty,
they are round and white,
they have a shell around them
that is a pretty sight,
I can eat them for breakfast,
I can eat them for lunch,
dont eat the shell,
or your teeth will go crunch

(by Aaron (age 7) and marvin
Druger)

Behind a Glass

A hungry lion at the zoo
Looking all around his pen,
Thinking very positive
That he will get his food again.

Just then a little girl walked by
And stared at the lion's mouth,
And the lion thought,
I will eat that girl without a doubt.

The lion ran toward the girl
But did not see the glass,
When he was five feet away
He saw he almost crashed.

The hungry lion now saw
That he was behind a glass,
He was to stay in his pen
And was not allowed to pass.

The best thing I can do
The lion thought,
When I see kids in a bunch.
Is to wait for the zookeepers
To come give me my lunch.
(Aaron Druger, age 13)

Stars

Small glowing balls
Twinkling in the night,
Visible at night,
Invisible during the day,
Raging with light.
(Aaron Druger, age 13)

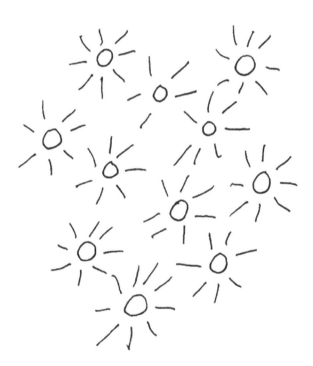

Life and Death

Having life is peaceful,
You can do all sorts of things,
Riding bikes and building blocks
And pretending you have wings.

Having death is sad.
You can't have any more fun,
You get very ill.
It means your time is done.

So when you're growing up,
Enjoy your life while you can,
'Cause…
   (Aaron Druger, age 13)

The Library Book

A single book sits on the library shelf
Waiting and waiting all by itself,
Knowing and knowing without a doubt
That someone will come to check it out.

The door opens wide, a young girl steps in
Checking books that are fat and books that are thin,
Until she comes to our book all by itself
Waiting alone on the library shelf.

The librarian checks it out like that
Marking the book with a purple thumbtack
And the little girl skips to a gnarled oak tree
Knowing she found a good book to read.
    (Keith Jamieson, age 11)

(I asked Keith why the last line doesn't rhyme. He
replied, "I got tired.")

Martin Luther King's Dream

People come in different colors,
They can be dark or light,
People come in different sizes.
But none are wrong or right.

No matter what the color
And no matter what the size,
Each of us is special
And our color's a disguise.

Martin Luther King said
That all people should be
Treated with respect
And with equality.

King told about his dream of
What the world would come to
   see.
That color makes no difference
When we judge ability.

King's life ended suddenly
When he was shot and killed,
'Though he tried his very best
His dream is unfulfilled.

But his mission will continue
Until society can bring
Respect for every person—
The goal of Martin Luther King.
(Rachel Druger, age 9, and
     Marvin Druger, age?)

Mr. Good

I'm Mr. Good,
I'm as good as can be,
If you need any help,
You can count on me.

When I fight with my sister
Like any kid would,
My parents remind me
That I'm Mr. Good.

I take out the garbage,
I make my own bed,
I say please and thank you
And make sure the dog's fed.

I clean all the dishes,
I mop up the floor,
I pick up the crumbs.
Can I do anymore?

Then everyone loves me
For the good things I do.
If you try very hard
Mr. Good can be You.
(Or Ms. Good can be too).
(Joshua Druger, age 11, and Marvin Druger, age?)

Mr. Bad

I'm Mr. Bad,
I'm as bad as can be,
If you need any help,
Don't count on me.

When I fight with my sister
Like any kid would,
I tell my parents
That I'm not Mr. Good.

I don't take out the garbage,
I don't make my own bed,
I don't say please and thank you
And don't care if the dog's fed.

I don't clean the dishes,
Or mop up the floor,
I don't pick up the crumbs,
I don't help anymore.

Then everyone dislikes me
For the bad things I do,
If you try very hard
Mr. Bad can be You.
(Or Ms. Bad can be too).
(Joshua Druger, age 11, and Marvin Druger, age?)

**Would you like to be
Mr./Ms. Good or Mr./Ms. Bad?
The Choice is yours.**

Poems by You

I wrote these poems
And so can you,
It's something
Anyone can do.

A poem does not
Have to rhyme
And you can
Write one anytime.

Think a thought
That's fun and new,
Then write the thought
And save it too.

Try to write a poem NOW,
When people see it,
They'll say…
"Wow!"

Roses are red,
Violets are blue,
Now I'm a poet
Just like you.

This is not really the end of this book. Poetry is Endless. So write your own poems on the following blank pages and add them to the book. Remember, a poem does not have to rhyme. It can simply be a thought put into words. Have fun writing your own poems. Everyone can be a poet.

Your Poems

About the Author

Why is Marvin Druger—a biologist and a renowned science educator—publishing a book of poems for children and adults of all ages?

His answer is, why not? Experiences leave lasting impressions, and Druger believes we enrich our lives by seeking as many different, worthwhile experiences as possible. His philosophy is that we learn from everything that we do, and everything that we do becomes part of what we are. We forget information, but we remember experiences. His poems focus on life experiences that are meaningful for adults and children. In his legendary general biology course at Syracuse University, he tried to provide meaningful, motivational experiences that enriched the lives of students and helped them identify their unique talents and where they fit in life. His life-size cutout at the Syracuse University Bookstore welcomes students to the world of books and scholarship.

Marvin Druger and his replica cutout
(courtesy of Steve Sartori)

Marvin Druger was chair of the department of science teaching, professor of biology and science education, and Laura J. and L. Douglas Meredith Professor for Teaching Excellence at Syracuse University. He retired in 2009 and is now a professor emeritus. He taught science for more than fifty-five years to more than forty thousand students and served as president of three international science education organizations—that is, the National Science Teachers Association (NSTA), the Association for Science Teacher Education (ASTE), and twice president of the Society for College Science Teachers (SCST). He also served as chair and secretary of the Education Section of the American Association for the Advancement of Science (AAAS). He has received numerous science education and teaching awards. In his retirement, he is a columnist for *Fifty-Five Plus* magazine (Druger's Zoo) and hosts a radio program on WAER-FM 88.3 (*Science on the Radio*). He also organizes and directs a Saturday Enrichment Program for Talented High School Students (Frontiers of Science) and does poetry readings for elementary school students and others. He also provides campus tours of Syracuse University for staff and students.

Printed in the USA
CPSIA information can be obtained
at www.ICGtesting.com
LVHW090413090224
771185LV00049B/998